CAN WE?

Comments and Recommendations
for Preserving Our Nation

GRANT REES

Order this book online at www.trafford.com
or email orders@trafford.com

Most Trafford titles are also available at major online book retailers.

Printed in the United States of America.

ISBN: 978-1-4269-7210-2 (sc)
ISBN: 978-1-4269-7209-6 (hc)
ISBN: 978-1-4269-7211-9 (e)

Library of Congress Control Number: 2011909281

Trafford rev. 06/08/2011

 www.trafford.com

North America & international
toll-free: 1 888 232 4444 (USA & Canada)
phone: 250 383 6864 ♦ fax: 812 355 4082

In Memory of my parents
and in appreciation of my teachers, family, and friends

PREFACE

There are dark clouds hanging over our Nation's Capitol as there are many dangers confronting our American Republic, including alternative voting methods and procedures, use of harmful and addictive drugs, running a Nation without a Congressional budget, natural disasters, involvement with foreign conflicts, uncontrolled public debt, uncontrolled boarders, costly and unfair campaign funding, unauthorized release of classified information, potential loss of outer space advantage, increased lobbyist pressure, degradation of religion, diminished family values, and dishonesty and bribery in government. CAN WE, as an American people, overcome these shortcomings and preserve our nation?

When we write letters, or send emails to our representatives in Congress, the usual response is a "position paper", and never a direct answer to our concerns. I realize that our elected legislators can not see much of their correspondence, but their staffs should categorize and brief our representatives, and forward our correspondence to applicable branches of government, or another cognizant representative.

The following email is indicative of our political campaigns:

"Grandma, do all fairy tales begin with 'Once Upon A time'?"

"No dear. There is a whole series of fairy tales that begin with 'If Elected I Promise'."

<u>We are tired of the same old political rhetoric</u> with little progress since the last political season. This frustration is compounded by the fact that the political season is getting longer and more expensive. I have been documenting my thoughts for several years, have written letters to the editor, and have sent numerous letters to our elected representatives; thus this book is a composite of many of these letters, as well as current issues. Nine amendments to the U. S. Constitution are among the many recommendations proposed. I hope that the comments, opinions, and recommendations presented herein will generate meaningful discussions and debates for viable solutions for the nation's present problems, and forestall some future problems.

Today's youth will be our leaders tomorrow. It is in the national interest that our citizens be prepared for life's responsibilities. Therefore I have included some thoughts relative to "Family Stewardship" for fostering the training of our youth. It is imperative that we insist that our schools teach U. S. History and certain "Life Skills".

Contents

COMMENTS AND OPINIONS

1. <u>Drug Use:</u>

Some States are considering legalizing the use of marijuana for the purpose of raising revenue.

The effects of legalizing marijuana:

a. Marijuana is much more addictive than nicotine; thus more smoking and more cancer.

b. Marijuana affects the brain and memory functions.

c. Legalized marijuana will increase the illegal use of more dangerous drugs.

d. When a substantial number of Americans are addicted to marijuana and other drugs, national security is at risk. Fewer Americans would qualify to serve in the military, etc.

e. Use of marijuana will drastically increase health costs.

A federal law should be enacted to make it illegal to grow, produce, sell, or possess marijuana in the United States. I believe that those who favor legalizing marijuana do not understand the long-term and short-term health implications.

2. Classified Information and National Security:

Some officials, at all levels of government, announce how they apprehended suspects, or disclose particular characteristics of a criminal or terrorist activity. The FBI should issue guidelines to Federal, State, and local officials on what type of investigative information which should not be disclosed to the public, and should be considered classified information.

There are numerous examples when such information was disclosed. This enables criminals or terrorist to escape detection for subsequent acts, or suggests to the terrorist ideas for future acts of violence. Here are a few examples:

a. An official stated, by name, several large cities which are the most vulnerable to terrorist's attacks.

b. Officials announced after the "911" (Setpember 11, 2001) attack that the hijackers had only bought one-way tickets, and checked no luggage. Do we need to educate the next bunch of terrorists what not to do, and disclosed their chararistic behavior to the public? Can we program our National Security computers with this type of information, as an algorithm? This same behavior was not detected on Christmas day, 2009.

c. Police and law enforcement officials and spokesmen give clues as to how they apprehended a suspect.

d. When the Health and Human Services Secretary resigned his cabinet position, he made this irresponsible remark: "For the life of me, I cannot understand why the terrorists have not attacked our food supply because it is so easy to do. We are importing a lot of food from the Middle East, and it would be easy to tamper with that."

e. Government officials said that the White House was vulnerable to radiological contamination such as anthrax. Do we really have to tell the world where we are vulnerable?

f. A Congressman suggests that there are vulnerabilities in train travel. Here again, any vulnerabilities should be discussed in closed sessions, and not for the purpose of political "posturing".

g. National security and intelligence was seriously compromised with the continuous disclosure of information relative to the death of Osama bin Laden. The lives of Navy Seals and foreign intelligent operatives have been put in danger. The fact that the Seals obtained documents, photos, and videos should have been kept secret, and the documents themselves should have been highly classified. Such irresponsible actions makes further intelligence more difficult. It appears that too many people are receiving intelligence information with no need to know. The President met with the Seal Team. I hope that there were no videos, photos, etc. of the Seal Team that might be leaked to the terrorists.

h. The WIKI leaks is another major scandal. It does not appear that the Justice Department is acting with any swiftness on prosecuting these cases. Compromising National Security and disclosing classified documents is a felony and must be prosecuted expeditiously.

i. **There should not be a debate in the news relative to torture. The United States does not torture its enemies.** Methods of interrogating enemies should be monitored by Congress oversight committee and the President.

Any information describing United States vulnerabilities or the characteristics of criminal activities should be highly classified. Likewise, any intelligence-gathering activities should also be highly classified.

It is easy for foreigners to acquire intelligence on U.S. operations because they can speak English. It is apparent that our government officials and the news media are excellent sources of information for our enemies.

3. Amendments to the Constitution

Amending the U. S. Constitution is a very serious business. But there is good reason to consider amendments. One method of proposing Amendments is by a Convention, but many fear this method, so a viable alternative should be considered to alleviate such fears. Unfortunately, a Convention may be required to propose such an amendment. Congress is becoming more polarized by the fact that re-election is their top priority; both major parties do nothing to enforce Federal laws, and thus puts some States in jeopardy. State's Rights are being diminished with every session of Congress. The elected State Legislators should be able to propose amendments and eliminate the Convention method of proposing amendments. With today's methods of rapid communications, and State's rights being quashed by the U. S. Congress, a much feared Convention is very likely unless we amend the Constitution as proposed herein.

The Constitution does not define the requirements for the U. S. Supreme Court. President Franklin D. Roosevelt tried to "stack" the court with fifteen justices., but his Judicial Procedure Reform Bill of 1937 was defeated. Thus the size of the court remained at nine justices per the Judiciary Act of 1869.

It is obvious that Congress will never consider a Terms Limit Amendment -- this is another reason to have an alternative to the Convention method to propose a Term Limits Amendment

Congress continually passes legislation for all Americans except themselves, and they reward themselves handsomely; thus a need for Congressional Benefits and Rights Amendment.

Congress has failed to provide a method to fill Congressional vacancies in times of national emergencies and other factors; thus a Filling Vacancies in the Congress Amendment is recommended.

The Electoral College has some flaws which should be considered in a Reformed Electoral College Amendment.

The Constitution does not require that a voter be a citizen of the United States, thus an Elections and Voting Procedures Amendment should be proposed. There are three basic criteria for a democratic voting methodology: (1) **the voter must be authorized and positively identified** as the one casting the ballot, (2) **the ballot must be secret**, and (3) **the ballot must be verifiable. If any one of these criteria is not ensured, the voting methodology is a failure and our democracy is in jeopardy.**

An amendment is recommended for overriding a Supreme Court decision within five years of such decision.

A controversial amendment is recommended for giving the legislative right to control pornography, and other sexual content. The people, through their elective representatives, should have a voice in the control of these materials and associated behaviors. The meaning of first Amendment is continuing to evolve in all aspects. I learned in school that the freedom of speech and the press were related to "political speech". I was not taught that it included pornography and sexual drug advertisements. Perhaps we should all read the entire Constitution, including the first amendment: "Congress shall make no law respecting an establishment of religion, or prohibiting the free exercise thereof; or abridging the freedom of speech, or of the press, or the right of the people peaceably to assemble, and to petition the Government for a redress of grievances".

Some in Congress are suggesting a "Balanced Budget Amendment" is needed. No such an amendment is necessary because there would be so many exceptions and loopholes that it would be ineffective. **A "Term Limits Amendment" would solve the budget problem!**

4.   Individual Identification and National Security:

American citizens are continually being profiled. Our credit card information tells where we shop, our buying habits, our location, our financial debts, etc. The Government's Internal Revenue Service collects information concerning our assets and liabilities. Programs like Google Earth, via satellites, show our property and our neighborhood. The internet is able to capture information about an individual from a life-time of activities. There are programs which describe our home, our property taxes, and the estimated value of our home. The U. S. Census Bureau collects information as to resident names, race, employment information, etc.; and the insurance companies and government agencies (e.g. Medicare) keep our health records.

But when it comes to National Security and authorized balloting, we find that many are opposed to a national identification card because of privacy arguments, though most of your personal information is already known.

Positive identification must be required at the polls, airports, etc.

5.   Immigration Issues:

Our government should ensure accurate tracking of aliens entering our country by land, sea, or air. Their visa time-limits should be closely monitored, along with their location.

The "National Register for clearing gun purchases" apparently does not contain a list of those persons who are registered aliens.

The Federal Government should reimburse the States for security, education, and medical costs incurred for undocumented immigrants or illegal aliens.

The construction of a security fence at our southern border seems ridiculous; miles of expensive fence, without surveillance, will not stop any invasion. The boarder patrol should have live satellite surveillance video with GPS coordinates, along with high tech sensors and barbed wire in desolate areas. The regular military should have shared responsibilities with the Immigration Service with several security stations along the border; I don' t believe this is a function of the National Guards. **Our borders must be made secure, and commerce and passenger vehicles must be thoroughly inspected**.

The Federal Government has not responded to the requests of the States relative to protecting invasions of their States. **Article IV, Section 4 of the U. S. Constitution states: "The United States shall guarantee to every State in this Union a Republican Form of government, and shall protect each of them against Invasion; and on Application of the Legislature, or of the Executive (when the Legislature cannot be convened) against domestic Violence."**

Social Security numbers and other documentation must be protected. It appears that private industry does a better job at protecting credit card numbers than the government does in protecting social security numbers. Employers must be honest and only hire or contract with persons with authentic documentation such as authentic social security numbers and other. Perhaps social security cards should be re-issued periodically with a photo.

It does not make sense to send undocumented aliens to their native country if they have been here for a period of time, or have families here. This is a case of shame on the Immigration Service, Congress, and employers.

Let's secure the borders, enforce employment laws, and finally grant citizenship to those who meet the citizenship requirements. Our country has had a great tradition of legal immigration, but politicians, federal agencies, employers, and others have ignored the lawful means. I sense that most of the undocumented aliens are good hard-working people. But **in today's world, we must ensure that drug traffickers and terrorists do not enter the United States.**

Community education classes should be offered for U. S. History, the U. S. Constitution, and the English language for those who are seeking U. S. citizenship, or for those who would like a refresher course in these subjects. We need transparency as to the process of legal immigration. Immigration quotas from various countries should be published, including the trends for the past ten or twenty years.

Let's identify who sets the quotas, and provide an assessment of future consequences as to the trends. What is the status of those refugees from Asian and Middle East countries when they are brought into the United States following warring conflicts or wars? We never seem to hear or read the answers to these questions.

6.   Strategic Importance of a Space Program:

If we sell our space and missile technology to other countries in return for our national debt loans, **the moon will be claimed by other countries and will be their strategic base. If a foreign country can control the outer space**, they can disrupt all communications in our country by knocking out our satellites. If this happens, the costs to recover will be prohibitive, financially and diplomatically; and our security as a nation will be at risk. We must NOT surrender the United States' leadership in space exploration. Our nation must continue have the capability to support our Space Station which is critical for research. **We cannot depend on other counties to solely support vehicles to reach the international space station; it is very risky.** We must make funding for our space programs a high priority.

A viable space program will ensure a future jobs market in science and technology and provide an incentive for studying math, science, and engineering courses. If there are no jobs, there will be fewer graduates in engineering and science, which will lead to fewer college offerings, and eventually leads to complete shutdown of future technology.

When we drastically downsize our nuclear and space industries, we lose experienced talent and experience that cannot be learned in the classroom.

7.   Military Preparedness

We should provide a new Universal Military Training and Service Act to require a statutory term of military service for men in order to alleviate the dependency of an all-volunteer military. This would make us better prepared for future contingencies, and ensure that our military has a good mix of skills to operate our high tech weapons, etc.

Present law requires almost all male U.S. citizens and aliens, living in the U.S., who are 18 through 25, to register with Selective Service. But why is this necessary? Shouldn't the Selective Service get records from schools, census records, etc? If a young man fails to register, will he get a draft call? Is this system fair, if some are cheating and not registering?

We should enforce all laws. I have never heard of any arrests of those who have not registered! We don't need any more personnel resources to enforce this law. Just a few advertised examples of enforcement in each State will to the trick. We should either enforce laws or rescind them.

Our Nation must be superior in Military hardware, and without apology.

8. Taxes and Political Campaign Donations

When I hear that some corporations and wealthy persons are not paying any taxes, I can only think that this is the fault of Congress -- too many loopholes in the tax code. Since there are many lawyers serving in our Congress, I can only conclude that they are either incompetent relative to legal issues, or they purposely "negotiate" loopholes into legislation for the purpose of getting it approved.

When we hear that some corporations are not paying taxes, yet paying millions to political campaigns, one must wonder if allowable political contributions should be based on a percentage of the taxes they pay.

At election time we hear the same old thing about "simplifying" the tax code. Who is actively working on a proposed bill? Simplification of the tax code would not necessarily put accountants out of work, rather it would allow more accountants to perform their auditing functions more thoroughly and effectively. The alternative minimum tax should be further adjusted upwards so as to limit loopholes.

Campaign financing needs to be revised. The period of soliciting and receiving campaign funds should be limited to one year prior to the election. We should also limit a candidate's own funds to $1,000,000.

9. Tort Reform

The awards for lawyers are excessive. Why should legal fees be based on the legitimate awards to the plaintiff, rather than actual legal costs and fair hourly rates? Punitive damage awards, if any, should not go to the plaintiff or to lawyers – the awards should go to society. Our Congress of lawyers like to tell doctors, bankers, business executives, and others what they are worth, but are silent relative to the earnings of their lawyer friends.

In some Radio & TV markets, nearly 15% of all advertising is by the legal profession: Attorneys dealing with IRS Tax issues, injury and accident claims, medical malpractice, drug related issues, felony defense issues, or selling legal software. What does this mean? Is the character of America changing? It used to be considered unethical for lawyers to advertise! Perhaps Tort reform is overdue. Lawyer fees are excessive.

A Bill should be passed to forbid punitive damage awards to go to lawyers or plaintiffs, to set limit of awards and lawyer fees, and control frivilous law suits.

10. Ignoring the U. S. Constitution

It seems that there is an increase of legislation that infringes on the U. S. Constitution. One example is the **new health care law** which is being challenged in the courts. Another example is the bill in Congress that would give **a U. S. Representative to the District of Columbia**. Article I, Section 2 of the Constitution states three qualifications for representatives: be at least twenty-five years old; have been a citizen of the United States for the past seven years; and be (at the time of the election) an inhabitant of the STATE they represent. For more than 200 years, the U. S. Congress has recognized this fact. A constitutional amendment is the only legal way to give the District of Columbia a voting representative.

If a **Treaty** can trump your right to have a gun, a treaty might also trump your other rights granted by the U. S. Constitution. How is Article VI of the Constitution interpreted? ("...The Constitution, and the Laws of the United States which shall be made Pursuance thereof; and all Treaties made, or which shall be made, under the Authority of the United States, shall be the supreme Law of the Land; and the Judges in every State shall be bound thereby, any Thing in the Constitution or Laws of any State to the Contrary notwithstanding.")

Also, **treaties are supposed to be approved by the U. S. Senate**. It seems that some agreements with countries are carried out as if they were ratified by the Senate.

"Education is what a fellow gets reading the fine print and experience is what he gets by not reading it"

------ **Author Unknown**

11. The Process of Drafting Legislation

The year 2009 has been a real civic lesson to many Americans who have been naive. We learned that our legislators, most of whom have law degrees, do not read, study, analyze, or honestly debate legislation before voting on it! We discovered that they are proud to announce that they have rules that allow the proposed legislation to be reviewed for three days prior to voting on it, regardless of the number of pages! Why would Congress, many of whom have law degrees, act so irresponsibly?

My "U. S. Government" classes in High School or College did not cover such things as "earmarks", or political "negotiations" tantamount to bribery.

Very lengthy bills are being written with hundreds or thousands of pages. The identity of the bill writers (a lobbyist organization, a congressional staff, etc.) is not known. The bills often have very extreme positions, which means that it takes many amendments to make the slightest change.

It would be better to have a small committee of moderates, and outside experts, meet in closed sessions, with no reporters or TV cameras. This committee can start with defining the problem, then discuss alternate solutions, and finally propose a bill. If the bill is moderate, it might have a chance of passing. Then the amendments will come to improve the bill, or at least consider other alternatives. This process would focus on solving the problem and keeping political considerations out.

Complex legislation needs reasonable time to "get it right". How many bills, with loopholes, have been proposed or approved by Congressmen who have law degrees? What about having a "Caucus of the Whole" and get it right.

The U. S. Constitution with all 27 Amendments is approximately 15 pages on standard paper size, and it took several months to work out the details, debate positions, etc. Now we see extremely lengthy bills and there is not sufficient time to read or analyze before scheduled limited debate and voting on the bill. The amount of time allocated to debating a bill should be based on its length -- perhaps a minimum of 1 day for every 20 pages of legislation, or what a competent lawyer would require.

Each legislative bill should be read and understood; then sufficient time allowed to make corrections. It is a fact that more often than not, "haste makes waste".

"You cannot help small men by tearing down big men.
You cannot bring about prosperity by discouraging thrift.
You cannot strengthen the weak by weakening the strong.
You cannot lift the wage earner by pulling down the wage payer.
You cannot help the poor man by destroying the rich.
You cannot keep out of trouble by spending more than your income.
You cannot establish security on borrowed money.
You cannot build character and courage by taking away man's initiative and independence.
You cannot help men permanently by doing for them what they could and should do for themselves."

Attributed to Abraham Lincoln

12. Federal Funding

a. Unused money near the end of a fiscal year is usually spent unwisely. The mindset is "Use the money or lose it". There has to be a better system to this antiquated system.

b. Government-sponsored Studies

It appears that research money is given to almost anyone who knows rudimentary statistics, and may not be qualified for basic research in any field. Many studies are merely statistical data, but no real science effort in the studies; for example, research on some diseases where almost all research is based on effect of certain drugs, but little research by those who know how to use a microscope.

c. Department of Education Funds

There should be some consideration for downsizing the U. S. Department of Education, and shift some responsibilities to the

States. A budget item could distribute most of the funds to the States, with absolutely no strings attached.

d.   Law Enforcement Expenditures

The FBI has spent millions of dollars on computer programs for identifying finger prints. A test of these computer programs could be performed by obtaining the finger prints of persons who had their finger prints taken by the military and/or a government agency, then submitting them to the FBI to see if they can identify the person. A live demonstration of Lie Detector testing would also be interesting.

e.   Accounting for CIA Funds

Has any one ever questioned how the CIA and Congress audits the accounts for the cash given to operatives or agents. Should the IRS audit active and retired agents, and Congressional members who are responsible for CIA oversight?

f.   Auditing Social Security Payments

Social Security payments to anyone 90 years of age should be verified whether the recipient is alive or deceased; and then virgorously prosecute when fraud is discovered.

g.   Government Savings Bonds

During World War II our government sold savings bonds to the American public, and were widely advertised. We are told that China holds most of our trillion dollar national debt, but no one seems to know the interest rate being paid for this debt! Shouldn't the American public have an opportunity to earn the same interest rate through savings bonds?

h. Foreign Aid

The United States does not seem to gain any friendship with the nations who receive our aid. Perhaps the nature of our aid should be limited to only food and medicine, and not weapons and money which enrich dictators or incompetent leaders. If the aid is not distributed to those who need it, without cost, then future aid should be discontinued. **There must be an accounting for any aid rendered. Continued aid should be predicated on whether a country is becoming self-reliant (also should be a goal of welfare systems).**

i. Federal Debt

Our lawmakers should present on paper where the budget cuts should be, and indicate the actual impact on those affected. If the cuts are fair, and across the board, it might not affect people as much as the political foes suggest.

13. U. S. Postal Delivery

With the increase of email and online banking, first class mail has dropped significantly. Fewer checks need to be written and and sent by first class mail. The Americans don't need mail delivery six days a week, three or four days would be sufficient.

In addition, the postal service still delivers mail door to door in older neighborhoods. I lived in a community for thirty-one years and nothing changed relative to mail delivery. Within a few blocks, there are four delivery systems: The older part of the neighborhood has door to door service. One block away from the door to door service, the mail boxes are required to be inside the sidewalk, so that the mailman (mail carrier) can walk down the sidewalk and deliver the mail rather than going door to door. A third method is only another block away where the mail boxes are required to be on the curb so that a mail truck can deliver the mail. Two or three blocks further, in a new area, there are group mail boxes with keys. Thus the homes and business that get door-to-door delivery have been subsidized by the other three delivery systems for more than a half century! It should be obvious what should be done to reduce postal service expenses. Delivery of mail to residential homes is antiquated and expensive. Group boxes should be installed in these neighborhoods.

Because of reduced first class mail, the postal service now puts junk mail advertising (loose newspaper ads) in your home mail box, and also in the rented boxes at the post office. This is a nuisance, and uses precious mail box space -- especially if one is paying for a rented box. These massive loose advertisements (with no addresses) can be a cause for lost mail.

14. Government Oversight

The government has many oversight responsibilities. But I'll just comment on one -- the Air Traffic Controllers.
Recent non-performance of air controllers has been limited to suspension, with pay! The non-performance is blamed on work schedules which has caused the controllers to fall asleep. I suspect that the real cause was using electronic devices such as iPods, ipads, and iphones -- listening to music (wearing ear phones), playing games, watching movies with earphones, reading a book, etc. We never had these problems before this technology came along. You would think that these devices would not be permitted when on duty as an air controller. I suspect that a local supervisor does not have authority to set work rules without approval from higher authority, or Union approval. You can bet that there will not be any serious discipline.

15. The News and Entertainment Media

The freedom of the press is very important for the survival of a democracy. The News media provides a role on "check and balances" on government. The news media must be honest, and not "agenda driven" or controlled by special interests. The news media plays an important role in keeping American citizens and Legislators informed on a wide area of issues.

Generally speaking, bureaucrats are not held to the same level of scrutiny as politicians. The news media has a unique role in probing these federal institutions and keep our legislators and citizens informed.

Several documentaries could be generated by the comments contained herein.

The news media could assume a more active role in monitoring mis-information on the internet and reporting factual information. Some internet sites try to "set the record straight"; however I've noticed that they sometimes gloss over essential information.

An example of inadequate information was the engraving of new presidential dollars without "In God We Trust" on the face of the coins. The Presidential Coin Act of 2005 permitted engraving the information on the edge of U. S. coins rather than on their fronts or backs. This may have been one of those laws that passed in Congress which was not read or debated.

16. Televising sessions of Congress

We see our legislators behind the camera when Congress is not in session, just delivering a political speech, placed in the Congressional Record, which is not read by our legislators, or anyone. Is it possible for a legislator, debating an important issue, to be able to influence the outcome of a proposed bill because of an honest presentation on the floor of Congress?

Why televise the speeches of our Representatives and Senators when there is not a quorum to conduct business? It appears that the legislators of both Houses of Congress just make campaign speeches for the TV cameras. Shouldn't there be a quorum so that the debates may reasonably influence a resolution of the problem being discussed? Shouldn't the purpose of "debate" be to change one's mind rather than present a party-line position? Can reason ever prevail? Also, it might be better to have a "caucus of the whole body" than special interest groups or parties.

17. Mass Transit Systems:

Legislation is required to layout plans for mass transportation systems throughout the nation. This would require setting aside land and right-of-ways for future construction. In many cases, we see home developments right next to major highways. This increases the cost of highways because of requirement for noise abatement, etc. It also uses land that could be used for future mass transportation systems such as high speed rail, subways, etc.

18. Washington Environment

The most dangerous legislative period is the 10 months following an election. That is why there is a push to get new bills passed (stimulus, health care, etc.) prior to September 1st. The rationale for this is simple --- it gives Congress a full year to dazzle the voters that their legislation was necessary, or possibly forget it. I think it is better for the country to have a "do nothing" Congress than to pass poor legislation.

A large percentage of our U. S. Representatives, Senators, and other elected officials have been indicted, investigated, or serving time in prison for criminal activities. Most, if not all, only regret that they got caught! Bribes are now called negotiations. Our elected representatives are bowing to specials interest groups, giving them money, and then receive a good portion of the money for their re-elections. One should wonder if all of these elected officials should be audited by the IRS -- a complete audit. Do you think they have Swiss bank accounts? It is highly probable that there is blackmail in politics.

I'm sure that freshman members of congress have been advised "to be careful at social functions, be cautious of the opposite sex, don't say or do anything for which you can be blackmailed, and thus be controlled. Actions speak louder than political rhetoric. There are people and organizations dedicated to find out everything about you".

19. "Political Correctness"

When "Political Correctness" trumps common sense, major problems occur like the massacre of American soldiers at Ft. Hood. Security should not mean "Political Correctness" in lieu of "Profiling" suspect groups of people until such potential threat no longer exists. Hiring more government employees or contractors cannot be a substitute for common sense profiling. Remember that terrorists bombed Pan Am Flight 103, the World Trade Center in 1993, the Marine Barracks in Lebanon, the military Barracks in Saudi Arabia, the American Embassies in Africa, the USS COLE, and destroyed the World Trade Buildings on 9/11/2001, the massacre at Ft. Hood, and the attempt to blow up a plane on Christmas day, 2009. **"Political correctness" is killing us.**

20. <u>Family Stewardship For Developing Our Youth</u>

Ideally our youth should learn self-discipline, responsibilities, work ethics, social and life skills, healthy habits, and the importance of education and service to others. Parents, schools, churches, day-care centers. their friends, and high profile individuals (e.g. athletes) have a significant influence in the "training" of our youth. Parents must be involved in monitoring all of these environments, and must set a good example. The parents and youth of some families just seem to co-exist in the same house with no family structure, and little interaction. or monitoring of their progress towards being an informed voter.

An **Appendix, "Family Stewardship"** offers suggestions to parents and guardians for nurturing their youth to be capable, responsible, educated, and independent citizens -- and to be informed voters at age 18!

21. <u>What Citizens or Prospective Citizens Should Know:</u>

Every citizen should know the basics of our country, and the workings of our republic. I believe that the teaching of American History is imperative for the preservation of our unique democracy. We must understand the principals upon which sustains our democracy lest we lose our democracy with series of subtle incremental changes. These basics should be learned in school, or community citizenship classes. For starters, I believe that **every voting citizen should know the answers to the following questions:**

1. What is the meaning of the American flag – the stars, strips, colors?

2. Who was the first President of the United States?
3. Who was President of the United States during the U. S. Civil War?
4. Who were fighting in the U. S. Civil War, and what were their causes?
5. Who is the President of the United States today?
6. Who is the Vice President of the United States today?
7. Who is the Speaker of the U. S. House of Representatives?
8. Who is the Majority Leader of the U. S. Senate?
9. Recite the Pledge of Allegiance to the United States.
10. Who is the Mayor of your city?
11. Recite the first verse of our National Anthem.
12. What is the name of our National Anthem?
13. Who wrote our National Anthem?
14. Recite the first verse of America (My Country 'tis of Thee)?
15. The tune of "America" is the same as the National Anthem of what country?
16. What is the name of your local news paper?
17. What slogan is engraved on our coins?
18. Are Federal Reserve Notes legal in the United States?
19. Who drafted the Declaration of Independence?
20. How many original colonies were there?
21. Where is Mount Rushmore? How many U. S. Presidents are sculptured on it? Who are they?
22. What is the history or meaning of the following holidays?
    Memorial Day
    President's Day
    Independent's Day
    Flag Day
    Martin Luther King Jr.
    Valentine's Day
    Mother's Day
    Father's Day
    Thanksgiving
    Christmas
23. When is Election Day?

24. How many U. S. Senators and U. S. Representative is your State entitled to?
25. What is the total number of U. S. Senators and Representatives?
26. Who are your U. S. Senators and U. S. Representatives?
27. What are the terms of office for U. S. Senators, U. S. Representatives, and President?
28. What is the Bill of Rights?
29. What is a Silver Certificate?
30. Who is the Commander-in-Chief of the U. S. Armed Services?
31. How old must one be to vote in the U. S.?
32. How do you register to vote in your county?
33. Does the U. S. Constitution require U. S. citizenship to vote?
34. When are young men required to register with the Selective Service?
35. What document did the U. S. Constitution replace?

If our schools are not teaching the answers to these questions, then we should be concerned and find out why.

RECOMMENDATIONS:

1. PROPOSED U.S. CONSTITUTIONAL AMENDMENTS:

a. PROCEDURE FOR AMENDING THE U. S. CONSTITUTION:

Comments:
There have been arguments against the Convention method of amending the U. S. Constitution: fear that it could completely overthrow the existing Constitution. But there must be a viable alternative to amending the Constitution. This Amendment eliminates the Convention method in favor allowing the elected State Legislatures to propose amendments to the constitution. A proposed Constitutional Amendment, either by the U. S. Congress, or by the State Legislatures, can only be ratified by the States, not by a Convention. This Amendment is considered so important that if Congress fails to propose this Amendment, then a Convention must be called for the specific purpose of proposing this Amendment.

Section 1. Article V shall be replaced as follows: "The Congress, whenever two thirds of both Houses shall deem it necessary, shall propose Amendments to this Constitution, or, two thirds of the State Legislatures propose Amendments to this Constitution, which, in either Case, shall be valid to all Intents and Purposes, as Part of this Constitution, when ratified by the Legislatures of three fourths of the several States."

Section 2. If the amendment is proposed by the State Legislatures, the subsequent ratification shall be a separate approval procedure, even if a State was one that proposed the Amendment.

Section 3. This article shall take effect immediately after being ratified.

b.   SUPREME COURT AMENDMENT

Comments:
The U. S. Constitution does not establish requirements for the Chief Justice and the Associate Justices, regarding age, citizenship, experience, etc. The Constitution does establish the minimum ages for Representative, Senator, and President as 25, 30, and 35 respectively.

Section 1. The United States Supreme Court shall consist of one Chief Justice and eight associate Justices. They shall be nominated by the President and confirmed by the Senate per Article II, Section 2 of the Constitution.

Section 2. A person nominated for the Supreme Court must be a natural born citizen of the United States, must be at least 45 years of age, and must have been a judge for a minimum of four years.

Section 3. A United States Supreme Court justice shall not serve beyond his or her 82nd birthday, except, justices who are serving at the time of ratification of this amendment shall be permitted to serve until the age of 85.

Section 4. This article shall be inoperative unless it shall have been ratified as an amendment to the Constitution by the legislatures of three-fourths of the several states within seven years from the day of its submission to the states by the Congress.

c. <u>TERM LIMITS AMENDMENT</u>

Comments:
Many believe that "Term Limits" should be decided at the ballot box; however, many party leaders discourage competition in the PRIMARY Elections; thus we have the same persons running in order to preserve seniority for powerful chairmanship positions. Many have served more than 30 years, and some over 50 years.

Section 1. A person may be elected to the U. S. House of Representatives a maximum of eight two-year terms.

Section 2. A person may be elected to the U. S. Senate a maximum of four six-year terms.

Section 3. Seniority in the House or Senate is based only on the time served in the respective house of Congress.

Section 4. This article shall be inoperative unless it shall have been ratified as an amendment to the Constitution by the legislatures of three-fourths of the several states within seven years from the day of its submission to the states by the Congress. Upon ratification, incumbents in House will be limited to twelve 2-year terms, and incumbents in the Senate will be limited to six 6-year terms. If they have exceeded these limits, they shall continue to serve until the expiration of their current term.

d. <u>CONGRESSIONAL BENEFITS AND RIGHTS AMENDMENT</u>

Comments:
The question arises as to why members of Congress exempt themselves from the very laws that they enact for all other citizens! And why should a member of Congress have full retirement benefits after serving only one term in office!

Section 1. Every member of Congress shall have the right to have his or her proposed legislation considered by the whole body of the legislative branch, with or without Congressional committee approval.

Section 2. Sessions of Congress may be televised, provided there is a quorum.

Section 3. Congress shall make no law that applies to the citizens of the United States that does not apply equally to the Senators and Representatives.

Section 4. Members or Congress shall not be eligible for retirement benefits unless they have served for a minimum of eight years as an elected member of Congress.

Section 5. This article shall be inoperative unless it shall have been ratified as an amendment to the Constitution by the legislatures of three-fourths of the several states within seven years from the day of its submission to the states by the Congress.

e. FILLING VACANCIES IN THE CONGRESS AMENDMENT

Comments:
In today's world of terrorists and nuclear proliferation, our nation must be prepared for all contingencies. As a result of the terrorist attacks on September 11, 2001, Congress spent six years drafting legislation that was flawed, including infringing on State's rights, granted by the 10th Amendment. The following proposed amendment includes the same provisions for Senators and Representatives.

Section 1. When vacancies happen in the representation of any State in the House of Representatives or Senate due to death, resignation, or legal removal from office, incapacity, disappearance, or hostage, the Governor of such State shall issue writs of election to fill such vacancies: Provided, that the legislature of any State may empower the Governor thereof to make temporary appointments until the people fill the vacancies by election as the legislature may direct; and provided that the remaining term of office is greater than 14 months.

Section 2. An individual designated, or elected for the remaining term of a Senator or Representative because of incapacity, disappearance, or hostage, shall serve until the Senator or Representative regains capacity, is located, and declares that he or she can resume office for the remaining term of office.

Section 3. During the period of an individual's service under section 2, the individual shall be treated as a Senator or Representative in Congress for purposes of all laws, rules, and regulations.

Section 4. In the event a catastrophe results in the death, incapacity, disappearance, or hostage of 87 or more Representatives, or 20 or more Senators, their replacements per section 1 shall not change the majority party as existed prior to the catastrophe until the next regularly scheduled election.

Section 5. Congress shall by law establish the criteria for determining whether a Senator or Representative in Congress is dead, incapacitated, or has disappeared, and shall have the power to enforce this article through appropriate legislation.

Section 6. This article shall take effect immediately after it has been ratified as an amendment to the Constitution by the legislatures of three-fourths of the several states within seven years from the day of its submission to the states by the Congress.

f.   REFORMED ELECTORAL COLLEGE AMENDMENT

Comments:
The present Electoral College elects the President and Vice-President by "electors" who are pledged to vote for particular candidates, as

prescribed by the various laws of the States and the District of Columbia. Under our current party conventions, the candidates for President and Vice President are selected to run as a team. This procedure can lead to some problems since Electoral College electors are not bound to vote in accordance with their "pledged vote". If neither the President/Vice President team receives a majority of the Electoral votes (270), then the decision goes to the House of Representatives (one vote per State) to elect the President, and to the Senate to elect a Vice-President. The time periods between the general election in November and voting by the electors in December, and the counting of the ballots in January creates a situation of uncertainty, anxiety, and possible mischief. Any national catastrophe during this time can cause further chaos.

This Amendment eliminates the election of electors, but instead assigns phantom electors, and the winner-take-all of the popular votes in each State and the District of Columbia. If there is not a majority of the elector votes, then the President-elect and Vice President-elect are the candidates with the greater number of popular votes by all States and the District of Columbia, provided that the candidates receive at least 35% of the popular vote. If not, then from the three teams receiving the highest number of electoral votes, the new House of Representatives (in January) would choose the President/Vice-President team, where each State has one vote, and the selection of President and Vice President is determined by the "team" that receives the most votes, and not by a majority, thus preventing a deadlock which could last for months. If the phantom elector votes were assigned proportional to the popular vote [accuracy only needed to one decimal], most elections would likely be referred to the House of Representatives and Senate to decide the President-elect and Vice-President-elect respectively. [This proposal amends Article II and Amendments 12, 20, and 23]

Section 1. Each state shall be assigned phantom electors, equal to the whole number of senators and representatives to which the state may be entitled in the Congress.

Section 2. The District of Columbia, constituting the seat of government of the United States, shall be assigned three phantom electors.

Section 3. The candidates for President and Vice President for each party shall be elected as a team, and both candidates must constitutionally be eligible for the office of President, and the President and Vice-President Candidates must not be a resident of the same State.

Section 4. The number of phantom elector votes assigned to each President/Vice-President team will be winner-take-all based on the popular votes in each State and the District of Columbia.

Section 5. If no President and Vice President team receives a majority of the phantom elector votes, then the President/Vice-President team which has the greater number of the total popular votes of the several States and the District of Columbia shall be the President-elect and Vice President-elect, provided that this team receives at least 35% of the popular vote; if not, then from the three teams receiving the highest number of electoral votes, the new House of Representatives (in January) shall choose the President/Vice-President team, but in choosing, the votes shall be taken by States, the representation from each State having one vote; a quorum for this purpose shall consist of a member or members from two -thirds of the States, the team having the greatest number of votes shall be the President/Vice-President elect.

Section 6. This article shall take effect immediately after being ratified as an amendment to the Constitution by the legislatures of three-fourths of the several states within seven years from the day of its submission to the states by the Congress.

ELECTIONS AND VOTING PROCEDURES AMENDMENT

Comments:
There are three basic criteria for a democratic voting methodology: (1) the voter must be authorized and positively identified as the one casting the ballot, (2) the ballot must be secret, and (3) the ballot must be verifiable. If any one of these criteria is not ensured, the voting methodology is a failure and our democracy is in jeopardy. If we allow internet voting, we can not be sure that the one voting is doing so of his or her own free will, and that the person is authorized to vote, or that the vote is secret. Moreover it would be difficult, if not impossible, to challenge the ballot, or initiate a ballot re-count. A wide-spread national computer virus on Election Day would be a major problem. With any kind of a software-driven voting methodology (voting machines or internet), there is always the possibility of some shrewd programming that could influence an outcome of an election; or a virus could change the results or cause the votes not to be counted.
The privilege of voting should be determined at least 30 days prior to an election, not just have someone drop in at a poll location and vote.

Section 1. Voters shall be U. S. Citizens and must be qualified to vote 30 days prior to an election per requirements established by the respective State laws.

Section 2. Internet or online voting shall not be permitted.

Section 3. Mail-in ballots shall not be permitted, except for persons out of the country. Other absentee ballots must be presented in person at places designated by the respective States.

Section 4. Voters shall show a picture-I.D. at the polling place.

Section 5. Voting machines shall be validated with the most sophisticated software available, and checked periodically at random.

Section 6. Voting methods shall ensure that ballots are **authorized, secret, and verifiable** in accordance with applicable State laws.

Section 7. Convicted felons shall never have the right to vote.

g.   Override Supreme Court Decision Amendment

Comments:
In recent years, the Supreme Court is being viewed by some as "legislating from the bench" in many cases, that is, they may not be ruling on "Constitutional grounds". Some have advocated a constitutional amendment which would over-ride a decision of the Supreme Court. This amendment requires that this "override" only apply to a decision that is less than five years old.

Section 1. Congress may override a U. S. Supreme Court decision by a vote of three-fourths of the members of both houses of Congress, provided that the decision is less than five years old.

Section 2. This article shall be inoperative unless it shall have been ratified as an amendment to the Constitution by the legislatures of three-fourths of the several states within seven years from the day of its submission to the states by the Congress.

h.   Anti-Pornographic. Lewd Acts Amendment

Comments:
It is understandable that politicians are reluctant to tackle Amendments to the Constitution, especially with the Bill of Rights; however, if we examine the social trends in our society, we must find ways to ensure a future society where there is common decency and respect for all.

Amendment No. 1 to the U. S. Constitution states: "Congress shall make no law respecting an establishment of religion, or prohibiting the free exercise thereof; of abridging the freedom of speech, or of the press; or the right of the people peaceably to assemble, and to petition the Government for a redress of grievances." The courts have interpreted "free speech and free press" to mean anything from lewd conduct and speech, to pornographic materials. Unless you are an American Indian on a reservation, you have no safe haven from smut.

This proposed amendment does not prohibit pornographic materials, but it does give the Federal, State, and local governments the right to control or eliminate pornography and associated sexual conduct, and control the advertisements of sexual materials.

Section 1. The Federal, State, and Local governments shall have the right to define pornographic materials and lewd conduct; and shall be empowered to restrict or regulate such materials or conduct, in any form, including electronic, written, television, radio, internet, bill boards, dress standards, or parades.

Section 2. This article shall be inoperative unless it shall have been ratified as an amendment to the Constitution by the legislatures of three-fourths of the several states within seven years from the day of its submission to the States by the Congress.

2. Copyrights

Our copyright laws have changed significantly. The well-known song, "Happy Birthday" was copyrighted in 1935, and could have been in the public domain in 1991. However Congress has changed the laws and now this song is still not in the public domain This song is really traditional in the American culture.

Congress needs to review the copyright laws, and at least initiate legislation to put "Happy Birthday" into the public domain.

The copyright for the U. S. National Anthem should be protected and disallow any other variations.

3. Lobbyists

No person who has served as a member of Congress or as a Congressional staff member, should not be permitted to be a lobbyist (registered or otherwise) for a period of five years following any term of office or service; and such person should not receive compensation, directly or indirectly, from another lobbyist, or lobbying firm during the same period.

4. Prohibit Payments for Using Tobacco in Movie or TV Scenes

The MOVIES have always been the best "advertising" for the tobacco companies. The existing tobacco laws do not make it illegal for a tobacco company to pay movie directors, producers, etc. for having a smoking scene in a movie! Have you ever seen a movie that does not have at least one smoking scene? These films really influence our young people to smoke, which puts their health at risk and drives of the cost of health care.

Congress must pass a law prohibiting the payments of any form, to movie producers, directors, actors, writers, or anyone associated with producing a movie film or TV program.

5. Ban the Use of Marijuana:

A Federal law is needed to ban use of Marijuana, as it is addictive and dangerous to one's health.

6. Scrutinize New and Old Laws:

How are the words in a bill protected from unauthorized changes as it is presented to Congress and later becomes law? There must be a responsible system to ensure that someone does not slip in extra language after it has been presented to members of Congress for a vote? Perhaps the news media could check on these matters.

Do the appropriate government agencies check payable accounts for accuracy? For example, are there computer algorithms to check such things as social security making payments to persons older than the national average, then verify that the persons are still living? Who is cashing the checks if payments are being made to deceased persons? A mandatory verification of social security payments should be made for anyone 95 years of age or older.

Old laws (e.g. 50 years or more) should be examined to see if payments authorized by them are still applicable, valid, or should be revised. "Let sleeping dogs lie" should not be the norm.

7. Process of Developing Good Legislation:

Each legislative bill should be read, understood, and allow time to make corrections. Implement a transparent process for writing legislation, and identify any "silent" supporters.

8. Postal Delivery:

a. Implement a program to **eliminate door-to-door residential mail delivery** over a six year period -- either install group mail boxes or mail boxes at the curb.

b. **Discontinue delivering unaddressed loose newspaper ads in all mail boxes.**

c. Deliver residential mail three days a week (half of residences on Monday, Wednesday, Friday; the other half on Tuesday, Thursday, Saturday)

9. Televising Congress

Televising members of Congress should not be permitted without a quorum present.

10. Tax Reform

Simplification of the tax code! (Have we heard this before?)

Adjust the alternative minimum tax upwards so as to limit loopholes.

Eliminate the so-called Bush Tax Cuts for those who earn more than two million dollars per year.

11. Space Program

Fund a Space Program to ensure that America continues to explore space for science, international cooperation, and national security purposes.

12. Military Preparedness

Provide a new Universal Military Training and Service Act to require a statutory term of military service for men in order to alleviate the dependency of an all-volunteer military.

13. Tort Reform

A Bill should be passed to forbid punitive damage awards to go to lawyers or plaintiffs, to set limit of awards, limit lawyer fees, and control frivilous law suits.

14. Establish a National Photo Identification card.

15. Campaign Financing

Campaign financing needs to be revised. Limit the period of soliciting and receiving campaign funds to one year prior to the election. Limit the use candidate's own funds to $1,000,000.

CONCLUSION

I received this email a few months ago with the title, "<u>Polluting our Language</u>":

"We have exploited the poor and called it the lottery.

We have rewarded laziness and called it welfare.

We have killed our unborn and called it choice.

We have neglected to discipline our children and called it building self esteem.

We have abused power and called it politics.

We have polluted the air with profanity and pornography and called it freedom of expression."

Whether you agree or not, it does indicate a division of thinking and values in our country. Thus, we as citizens must study the issues and determine what policies are good for the preservation of the United States of America. We must be honest in our jobs, with our associates and friends, and with ourselves. Honesty and fairness is absoltely necessary for good government and personal relationships.

CAN WE AMERICANS PRESERVE OUR NATION?

"Train up a child in the way he should go:
and when he is old, he will not depart from it."

Proverbs, 22:6

APPENDIX: FAMILY STEWARDSHIP

Introduction

Each of the various species of animals has a period of time to wean their young from the parents, the time varying from a few days to a year or more. The human species requires the longest period, approximately 18 years (voting age per the 26th amendment), and even at that, the training does not end. This "weaning" period is divided between home, schools, churches, day-care centers, and the general social, and now "entertainment" environment. Parents, schools, churches, and day-care centers are all involved in the training of our youth. Parents must be involved in monitoring all of these environments. The parents and youth of some families just seem to co-exist in the same house with no family structure, and little interaction or monitoring of their progress towards being an informed voter.

Some areas of family stewardship and training are presented for "weaning" our youth to be responsible young men & women. They are not meant to be all inclusive, nor are they listed in a priority order.

1. <u>Family Rules</u>

   · Time for bed times, meals, family meetings, practice musical instruments, physical fitness
   · Appropriate age for certain activities with friends
   · Limits on game time & other entertainment (computers, electronic "gadgets")
   · Work (chores, study, music practice, & other family responsibilities) before play
   · Conditions for driving the family car
   · Eating between meals
   · Spending limits; allowances
   · School work (homework)

2. <u>Family Responsibilities and Chores</u>

   · Keeping room and bathroom neat; make bed, organize desks and drawers
   · Clear dinner table, rinse dishes, load dishwasher or wash dishes; unload dishwasher
   · Vacuum carpets; sweep floors, clean woodwork, dust
   · Clean or help organize rooms, garages, etc.
   · Care for pets: Feed pets (dogs, cats, fish, etc.); walk the dog; pick up droppings
   · Cut and trim lawn; sweep sidewalk and patio; water lawn
   · Plant, weed, and water garden
   · Value of work: learning skills, responsibilities, promptness, dependability, teamwork
   · Discipline to study & learn, to work with others, etc.
   · Shoveling snow or cleaning sidewalks, driveways, or garage floor
   · Home repairs
   · Laundry

3. <u>Family Traditions</u>

- Religious or ethical value teachings. A long-time cliché: "A family that prays together stays together"
- Family activities: regular family meetings, table games, vacations, camping, hiking, biking, skiing, table games, music, etc.
- Family traditions for holidays, birthdays, etc.
- Family goals
- Family pride in the outward appearance of home and yard
- Good deeds for our neighbors and service to our communities

4. <u>Family Safety and Emergency Plans</u>

- Family Plans in case of Fire, Flooding, Lightening, and other emergencies
- Children and Strangers
- Learning First Aid and location of emergency kits
- Safety around house; handling flammable liquids; campfire safety, etc.

5. <u>Family History & Genealogy</u>

- Learn family genealogy and history
- Encourage writing a personal diary or journal
- Learn stories of ancestors; View pictures of ancestors.

6. <u>Social Skills</u>

- Table Etiquette: setting the table, selection of eating implements
- Writing thanks-you notes
- Meeting and addressing gentlemen & ladies
- Dinner conversation

7. <u>Health, Diet, and Exercise</u>

- Drugs, smoking, hearing loss, sex, bad habits
- Personal hygiene
- Physical exercise

8. <u>Education</u>

- Monitoring and assisting children's school assignments
- Exploring various vocations
- Patriotic issues (U.S. Constitution, Declaration of Independence, National Anthem, and responsibilities of citizenship, Pledge of Allegiance)
- Supporting schools, PTAs, attending teacher's conferences

9. <u>Do Our Youth Know the Answers to these Questions</u>?

Who was the first man to walk on the moon?
Who invented the Light Bulb?
Who is credited with inventing the Television?
Name a major college football team and its coach.
Name two major collegiate sports.
How often should the oil be changed in your car?
What is a MP3 player and an IPOD?
How many inches are there in a yard?
How long is an American football field?
If a Boy Scout, repeat the Scout motto, slogan, Oath, and Scout Law.
Who has the right-of-way at a 4-way or all-way Stop sign?
Who was the first athlete to run a mile in less than 4 minutes?
What is the average speed in miles per hour if a mile is run in exactly four minutes?
If the score is 4 to 3 at the end of the ninth inning in American baseball, how many more innings need to be played?
Name the positions on a baseball team.

Name two clefs of a musical score.
Name one major play written by William Shakespeare.
Name one major composition by J. S. Bach.
Name two operas.
Using middle C as a reference, which pitch is higher, C# or Cb?
What causes the tides?
What are the freezing and boiling point temperatures for water in degrees Fahrenheit and Centigrade at sea level?
Name at least one Jewish holiday.
Where in the Bible can you find the Ten Commandments?
State four beliefs of your religion?
What advice, relative to religion, did President Washington give in his Farewell Address?
What are the first five books of the Bible (Old Testament) called?

10. Life Skills

- Cooking
- Musical skills
- Home repairs and maintenance
- Knitting, crocheting, sewing, making clothes, ironing; home-cleaning skills & procedures
- Sports: swimming, tennis, bowling, skiing, golf, skiing, racquetball, etc.
- Gardening and lawn care; learning to plant, prune shrubs & trees, etc.
- Reading good books
- Vehicles: driving with responsibility and learning how to maintain vehicle relative to safety and maintenance.
- Family finances, budgeting, debt management, interest rates, prudent investing, credit cards, checking accounts, reconciling bank statements, life insurance, auto insurance. **This should be taught in our schools.**

Have our youth ever seen a family budget?

Family Budget

BUDGET ITEM	Month	Annual		BUDGET ITEM	Month	Annual
Mortgage or Rent				Gifts/Other		
Property Ins.				Life Insurance		
Property Taxes				Long-Term Care		
Maintenance				Phone		
Utilities-electric, etc				TV		
Gas (heat, etc.)				Internet		
Groceries				Newspaper, etc.		
Clothing				Tuition		
Medical Insurance				Books/Supplies		
Health Products				Emergency Fund		
Prescriptions				Investments		
Auto Insurance				Entertainment		
Maintenance				Memberships		
Registration				Travel & Vacations		
Fuel (vehicles)				Hobbies		
Auto Loan				Dining Out		
Credit Payments				SUB-TOTAL 2		
Church donations				SUB-TOTAL 1		
SUB-TOTAL 1				GRAND TOTAL:		

"... Of all the dispositions and habits which lead to political prosperity, religion and morality are indispensable supports. In vain would that man claim the tribute of patriotism, who should labor to subvert these great pillars of human happiness, these firmest props of the duties of the men and citizens. The mere politician, equally with the pious man, ought to respect and to cherish them. A volume could not trace all their connections with private and public felicity. Let it simply be asked: Where is the security for property, for reputation, for life, if the sense of religious obligation desert the oaths which are the instruments of investigation in courts of justice? And let us with caution indulge the supposition that morality can be maintained without religion. Whatever may be conceded to the influence of refined education on minds of peculiar structure, reason and experience both forbid us to expect that national morality can prevail in exclusion of religious principle..."

From George Washington's "Farewell Address"

ABOUT THE AUTHOR

Grant Rees was raised in Reno, Nevada. He graduated from Reno High School, the U. S. Naval Academy (B.S.), the U. S. Naval Postgraduate School (MSEE), and American University (MBA). He and his wife have raised two sons. He has resided in Nevada, on Navy Ships, California, Vietnam, Oregon, Maryland, Idaho, and Utah.